Nilufar G. Karkhiran Khozani
Romance Would Be a Very Fine Bonus Indeed

Nilufar G. Karkhiran Khozani

Romance
Would Be a Very Fine
Bonus Indeed

Tinder-Sonette

re:sonar verlag

Bibliografische Information der Deutschen Bibliothek

Die Deutsche Bibliothek verzeichnet diese Publikation
in der Deutschen Nationalbibliografie; detaillierte
bibliografische Daten sind im Internet über
https://portal.dnb.de abrufbar.

Erste Auflage 2020
re:sonar verlag
ist ein Imprint des Wehrhahn Verlags
www.resonarverlag.com
Umschlaggestaltung: Anna Flügge
Satz: Carl Philipp Roth
Druck und Bindung: Sowa, Piaseczno

For all the lovers left alive

Flockige Milch im Kaffee
Ordnungsamt
Interessante Geschäftsmodelle
Am besten hast du schon getrunken, wenn wir
    uns treffen

We have travelled the depths of love
Within ourselves
With each other
Stripping back social conditioning

Life is very simple
No cats, just love
Über mir ist die Decke

Knife emoji
Chain emoji
Pill emoji

— Auf der Suche nach 'nem
Schlagbohrer

Auf der Suche nach 'nem Schlagbohrer
I don't mean to scare anyone
Need some more love
Kind and/or pissed off

It appears I'm very soft
I'm not cool, just short sighted
Anwendungstechniker
Mermaid emoji

People who are
Passionate about something
Chocolate, cleaning, family

LOVE
LIVED
LIKE

— Feeling Feelings

Feeling feelings
Kind of deep
Abstract lover
Tiny but trouble

Admirer of pastel tones
Highly concave spoons
Knots, socks, raincoats
Dabei über Hummus reden

Oh hey!
Looking for coke!
Ok?.

98% Nope
1% Meh
1% OMG

— Based in Berlin

Based in Berlin
Interested in saving the world
Interested in a new world
Auch auf Deutsch

What you see is what you get
Alles kann, nichts muss
Qui baise qui
Come as you are

The anticipation of a first kiss
Jajaja
Ich flaniere lieber durch die Welt
Und genieße die Realität

Sorry, not sorry
I write for money

— Floral Patterns

Floral patterns
Nur was mechanisch funktioniert
Katzen sind mir sympathischer
Aufrecht, weise und stabil

Zum ersten Mal, also…
All passive
And if one can flirt at all in German
I'm open to exploring my vocabulary

ONS
0815
Tech startup

Wolfenbüttel
Busy people
Superheroes

— Hello and Welcome You Wonderful Creation!

Hello and welcome you wonderful creation!
Got a kick drum beating in my chest
There is just so much I want to do
Lass mal Kaffee trinken gehen

We're sharing chewing gum
And comparing socks
Somebody out there for mental high-fives?
Oder mit Haus am Meer?

Work in progress
Looking for anything that makes me feel
Tbh

Emotionally available humans
Flying
Die Lüge kann die Gegenwart retten

— Milchmädchen

Milchmädchen
Happy girls are the prettiest
Kritisch
Lebt gerne so als würde gerade ein Film gedreht

Mag auch Passivitäten
Manchmal musst du nur atmen
Gehöre zu der guten Seite der Macht
Rechtschreibung meets Wortfindungsstörung

Du bist eine Prinzessin
Oder suchst eine?
Platonisch
Die drei F's

Wer A sagt muss gar nix
Und ich sag Rock'n'Roll

— Geh mir weg mit Yoga

Geh mir weg mit Yoga
My hair is indeed naturally blue
Lover of contemporary art
Toilet emoji

People say I'm entertaining tho
Mulan after her Britney moment
Klarname
Blurred face

Let's get tipsy and touchy
Das ist vielleicht nicht das Leben
Das ist ein Silberstreif

New people
Or a ghost
Magisches Theater

— Wir sind brutal heiß

Wir sind brutal heiß
Here to look at shirtless mirror selfies
Victory emoji
Also bei Obi gibt es das nicht

5'7
But I
Identify
As 5'11

If you're only looking for a place
To stick your dick in
I heard cactuses have
Quite pleasurable holes

We must get together
At least once in our lives

— Bored of Swiping

Bored of swiping
So sometimes my friends swipe for me
Curvy flesh
Bring Schokolade mit

Deep talks about awareness
Alles oberflächlich
I showed you my dick
Pls respond

Ananas ist die neue Mango
A tough girl
These two art forms dominate
About 80% of my existence

Let's hang out
And do something we haven't done

— One of Those Arty Broke Bitches

One of those arty broke bitches
Loner
Queen of doom
Aszendent: Straße

Hopefully food
Won't disappoint me
Like you did
Let's get serious

Not really there
Transformative world
Berlino
Schule des Lebens

I love my routines
Romance would be a very fine bonus indeed

— No Sex Currently

No sex currently
I had three nuns
Come to my house the other day
They have given me my virginity back

I'm yellow and made of rubber
I tell lame jokes
Ich bin intelligent und gebildet
Wäre gut, wenn du da mithalten könntest

Feinsinnige Männer
Frauen, die Fleisch essen
Sanctuary in Berlin

Krisensicher
Acts of kindness
La felicidad es el deseo de repetir

— Fat

Fat
Up for massage exchanges
Don't seem to get enough of the chaos
Which artisan sex toy are you?

I like dancing with my hands in the air and my
    eyes closed
Aimless wandering
Be honest, be kind
Und persönlich zu wachsen

A mix between power ranger and Pippi Long-
    stocking
If you like traveling, what are you escaping from?
Lately been feeling like a comic character
Living in multiple universes

Wir sind sehr glücklich und würden das gern mit
    dir teilen
Pizza emoji

— Looking for Everything And Nothing

Looking for everything and nothing
Whiskey bourbon rum
A cute alien to kiss
I would also love to play tennis

Fantastic daydreamer
Hot and cold
Here to find true and everlasting love
No tourists

Full sentences upon EU marriage
No games no drama
Smoker for the next three years
Hunter for the bargains

Baby, I'm bored
And likely wasting your time

— Wild Horses Run Faster

Wild horses run faster
Lifelover
Maybe I fall in love
Maybe I'll fall in a dumpster

Was festes
Tiefe Intellekt Sinnlichkeit
Vielleicht auch knutschen
Picture of a chewing sheep

Wie bin ich?
Berlin, 172
I'm a fish and a bird
I'm not going to leave any time soon

I want a husband and kids!
Anything not leading to that is a dealbreaker

— What's Your Apocalypse Game Plan?

What's your apocalypse game plan?
What makes you special?
Glitter
Teeth

Sydney, Melbourne, LA
NYC, Toronto, Vancouver
Chicago, Barcelona, Lissabon
Avoid bad company

Nichts zu kompliziert
Survivor of the daily confusion
Suburbia
Living life without concepts

#mff
#onlyshaved

— My Mom Wants Me Out of the House

My mom wants me out of the house
So she can put my room on Airbnb
Ich bin ein schwieriger aber glücklicher Sonderfall
    und
Neu in der Gegend

Trying not to be a hermit
Überfordert mit der Selbstdarstellung
Basically I enjoy life
Let's go to the park

Night on the planet
Die Route wird neu berechnet
Don't hesitate sending nudes
If they have good composition and lighting

Schwuppdiwupp Kartoffelsupp
Damn, I wish I was your lover!

— Auf der Suche nach Verbindlichkeit

Auf der Suche nach Verbindlichkeit
Auf der Suche nach den Sternen
On a spiritual quest
Beer emoji

Kinky bitch
Social justice witch
Wildly disappointing
Pretentious as fuck

Superlikes are 100% accidental
I like people with a brain
Bevorzuge aber deutsch

Not looking to be your wife
Nor the mother of your children
And even less yours

— Burner, Lover, Playful

Burner, lover, playful
Curious
Present
In it for the joy

Doch eher dominant
Boundary pushing
Keine Brieffreundschaften
I am really, really cool, you know

Mature enough to stay away
From games
Fun, sex & booze

Crazy ideas over coffee
Dopamine
The thrill

— Short Random Stories

Short random stories
Thinkers and lovers
In all shapes and forms
Theater of the oppressed

Nur die Schönen
Die mit der Seele aus Gold
Grundsätzlich müde und hungrig
Deal with it

Zeitlich nicht orientiert
Space is not just a place for stars
Whatever flows comfortably and naturally
Überrasch mich

Dirty talks is poetry
Always inappropriate

— Tierdokumentationen sind meine
große Leidenschaft

Tierdokumentationen sind meine große Leiden-
    schaft
You must be a good kisser
Du bist gut, wie du bist
Schreibe mir nicht, wenn du Angst hast

Blond
Sun goddess
Ozean
Gern mal feminist killjoy

Blaue Augen
Boom chakalaka
Blablabla

Wir sind lebensfroh
Spiel und Spaß
Lalala

— Krass, ist das schlimm hier

Krass, ist das schlimm hier
Keep it that way
Heeling and growing
I will judge your tattoos

Ja
Ich suche nach einer Frau
Wie sie genau sein soll
Weiß ich noch nicht

Interessant
Besonders
Bei Edeka
Don't be hard on me

Not really into
The leftovers of your heart

— Chatten macht mich total nervös

Chatten macht mich total nervös
Ich suche eine süße Frau
Die mich so nimmt wie ich bin
I want effort

Bisschen Kölscher Proll
Bisschen Kultursnob
Schattenanbetend
Mein Herz ist schwarz wie deine Coca Cola

Die Distanz zwischen Traum und Wirklichkeit
Klein und dick
Schöne Begegnungen

Insanitizing my surroundings
With poetry
Lipstick emoji

— I Love Sleeping

I love sleeping
Movies about troubled teenagers
Into politics and lesbianism
It's ok to google it

I don't like extremes
Sportverletzungen
Willing to be more social than normally
Write me if you are better than pizza

Not mass produced
Brain emoji
Yes really

Alles wird schön
Wenn die Sonne drauf scheint
Yeah right

— I'm Not a Sociopath

I'm not a sociopath
But I unnerve people in the same way
Sportliches Energiebündel
Bear with me

Harry Potter
Cis men
Twenty years from now
You will be more disappointed

43 not 37
Getting lost in wild places
My female intuition
Is currently unavailable

Treffe gern nette Menschen
Und falsche Entscheidungen

— Be Optimistic

Be optimistic
But stay realistic
Let me take a picture of you
In a not-at-all alphabetical order

Picture with cat
Picture with sunglasses
Picture riding a bike
Arroganz auf zwei Beinen

Fast verheiratet
Fake Gespräche
Feminismus

Don't take it personal
If it takes some time
To get back in the game

— Invite Me to Your Party

Invite me to your party
Elephant emoji
Not interested in being objectified by anyone
The grass is greener where you water it

Frauliches Weibsbild
Egal welchen Geschlechts
The hating part
Würde gern mal wieder Pilze sammeln gehen

Let's go to a concert
And talk about
How we're disappointing our parents
Whatever works

Romantik
Die habe ich längst überwunden

— A Night Is Not Nice

A night is not nice
Without madness
Lots of rattle lab accidents
Ein guter Anfang

To those who are reading this
Do not fall in love with ideas
I'm a bad girl
I want heartache more than sex

We are kinky and open minded
Kind of neurotic
My fat keeps me warm
Always

Der Satz mit den instabilen Ikeamöbeln
Und der emotionalen (In)Stabilität

— Interesting People I Guess

Interesting people I guess
Insects and stories
Zero waste
The kid is not my son

You look like trash
May I take you out?
Sonst bin ich sehr lustig und rede gerne
We're all going to hell anyway

Out of office
Living life
Jetzt mit 30 Tage Geld-zurück-Garantie
An der eigenen Version festhalten

Die Würde des Menschen
Ist auch beim Ficken unantastbar

— Hey Everyone!

Hey everyone!
Seriously though, not here for dating
DJ Horny offline
Oscar Wilde quote

Before I was an adult
I was a little wreck
Keine Erwartung
Keine Enttäuschung

Eigentlich eine gute Partie
European royal families
Marketingkommunikation
Elysium

Ich hoffe, dass es nicht zu arrogant klingt
Isst das letzte Stück Höflichkeitsschokolade

— Made of Star Stuff

Made of star stuff
I like art films
Video games
And prohibition era cocktails

Mermaid at heart
Straightforward
Quite sweet but quite militant
Decided by sudden death

Back on here for plain boredom
Frankly
Time to live a little

No impulse control
What you seek is seeking you
The only valid answer

— Es ist noch babyblauer Sand auf meinem Thron

Es ist noch babyblauer Sand auf meinem Thron
Schwer ruht das Haupt
Was die Krone trägt
Picture of a chicken

Business consultant
Something with art
Tell me what's wrong with you!
Aber bitte kultiviert und nicht so plump

Not my cat
Not my llama
Löwenbändigerin
Rainbow emoji

I'll give you the moon
If you give me ur-anus

— I'm Like Marie Curie But Stupid

I'm like Marie Curie but stupid
People find me likeable
Posing with African orphans
Hands down, I'm pretty histrionic!

You look like my next mistake
Nicht wundern, falls meine Schwester antwortet
Dafür bekommst du mich
Holocaust memorial selfie

All my friends died in an accident
I sometimes need new ones
Rechtskonservativer neoliberaler Wählertypus
Führerschein und Auto vorhanden

Nazis nerven mehr als Wespen
German flag emoji

— Dealing With Words And

Dealing with words and
Wild ponies
I do smile
I do bite

Trial and error
Tendency to unpredictable behavior
Erratic changes of mood
But lovely

Tongue twister
Jokes
Interpreting dreams
And magician tricks

Ich mag Bier
Schreib mir

— Chubby bunny

Chubby bunny
Austherapiert
Neu hier
Did I miss anything?

Silliness
Quantum physics
Ehrlichkeit und den Humor deiner Mutter
I'm objectively one of the best people

Wo sind'n hier die Kanacken
Oder gibt's für uns eine extra App
Von der ich nichts weiß?

Ihr dürft gern rauchen, saufen
Fleisch essen
#Knutschenistwichtigeralshitler

— Make Your Bed, Be Kind

Make your bed, be kind
Don't be shy to tell me your fantasies
Talk about lucid dreaming
Seifenblasen sind immer 'ne Option

Don't tell me you prefer black women
Mercy
I am wearing swimsuits
Doesn't mean I want to fuck you

Wiser than the images suggest
Which after all these streets is yours
I heard you like bad girls
Well I'm bad at everything

I guess it's the honeymoon phase
This is where love comes to die

— Lebensfrohe selbstbewusste Frau

Lebensfrohe selbstbewusste Frau
The nature & me
Non smoker
Dog lover

Lieber Hirn als Muskeln
Lieber draußen als drinnen
Lieber Liebe als Angst
Picture of sunset

Very tired
Das schöne Wetter im Sommer muss unbedingt
    genutzt werden
I don't care what you carry in your pants
Like really

Jenseits von richtig und falsch liegt ein Feld
Dort warte ich auf dich

— Dominant Character

Dominant character
Cyborg
Tired and gay
Always feel like dancing

Wir flechten Körbe und so
Vermutlich nicht, was du erwartest
Im not the perfect one
But I'm the one with heterochromia

Sara
Lola
Jennifer
Ich auch

Du warst hier
Und wir war'n frei

— Ein intellektueller Spaßvogel

Ein intellektueller Spaßvogel
Couch – Party – Strand
Die ganz alten analogen
Hast du ein Hausschwein?

Ich irre durchs Leben
Creepy & honest
Steal your girl
Just for fun

Es ist eine Perücke
Scheisz auf deinen maskulinen Standard!
So why don't I have a girlfriend?

In Berlin for today
Hauptsächlich auf der Suche nach Sex
Auch wenn ich da voll unsicher bin

— Nur weil ich Femme bin

Nur weil ich Femme bin
Heißt das nicht
Dass ich nicht rotzig bin
Ach ja, und ich habe Probleme mit der
     Kommunikation

If I was allowed a longer profile
Energy flows
I will lead
If you are willing to follow

Aber generell halte ich nicht so viel
Von dieser Nähe-Hierarchie
Auch Biertrinken kann sehr intim sein

Wenn du meinst, du hättest das Recht
Zu wissen, was ich in der Hose hab
Verpiss dich!

— Konfetti

Konfetti
Soft heart
Espresso
And of course business networking

Well fuck me
It's that time of year
Trustful, honest, reliable
No handstands

Despite myself
I do not feel ashamed
Cuddling after sex doesn't mean falling in love but
Treating us as humans

Text me if you're into stupid jokes
We are all just stories in someone's book

— Süßes Mädel

Süßes Mädel
Fitness girl
Fräulein Wunderlich
XL Frau

Zukünftige Weltverbesserin
Naturstoned
Kauffrau für Bürokommunikation
Dressed up as witch

Film und Fernsehen
Weizenbier
I know it's wrong
Whatever

Ich möchte mein Leben teilen
Nicht aufgeben

— Please Don't Give Me What I Want

Please don't give me what I want
Feminine Frauen
Und hübsche Männer
Nicht-suizidale Philosophie

Intellekt darf aber nicht arrogant sein
Auch ein hey wie geht's dir
Ist erlaubt
Da sind mehr Details

Two cosmic butterflies
Rote Pandas und Wasserschweine
Stranger things
Mau Mau spielen bei Waffeln und Gin

Ansonsten flasht mich einfach
Our social reality

— Ergotherapeutin

Ergotherapeutin
Lesen und schreiben
Essen und Sport
Clapperboard emoji

Feurige Südländerin
Ich
Es hat noch nie geschadet
Shakespeare quote

I always have warm feet
Open source
Für eine neue Erfahrung

Moin moin
Ruby ruby ruby
1234

— Fachhochschulreife

Fachhochschulreife
Münchner Kindl
Für schwache Nerven nicht geeignet
Eins davon ist gelogen

Kaufe nichts
Ficke niemanden
Erzählt bitte nicht meiner Oma davon
If you're not ready to talk

Grüße an alle Jodler
Die meinen
Über mich schreiben zu müssen

The kind of people
Who force you to
Level up in everything you do

— Level 1

Level 1
Ich schau einfach
Was hier so los ist
Sag ich nicht

Wurde von meinen Freunden im Garten vergessen
Schade
Picture of skeleton
Meine Katzen knabbern manchmal an mir

Lagerfeuer
Lüneburg
Out of your league

Hallo
Ich bin Franzi
Und wie sie nicht alle heißen

— Sixpacks sind unbequem

Sixpacks sind unbequem
A good conversation
Or no talking at all
Emotionally detached

Please spare me
I'm a hedgehog
That was lost in the fog
But won't go back

As deep as you can dig
I've never said I was an angel
No drama
But I keep my eyes open

Always ambitious
Always restless

— Nachhaltigkeit

Nachhaltigkeit
Bewusstes Leben
Kein Selfiemädchen
Nun habe ich doch den Mut

Not here for your horny boyfriend
Hiding on your 10th photo
Not today
Ich bin müde

Herrin der Leichtbekleideten
Superfunny
A bit shy

Zebra emoji
Red bull
We're game!

— Enthusiastic Pervert

Enthusiastic Pervert
Questioning and curious
Craving the void
The pirate ship ride completely terrifies me

Nur für Verrückte
Die aus privaten Gründen hier sehr rar sind
I'm very passionate about going to bed early
And free vet advice

Im Flixbus zwischen Hamburg und Berlin
Wir sind neugierig
Grün
Du zahlst!

Prove you are not dead
And please don't live 126268288+ km away

— #anti-you

#anti-you
Vielleicht weil ich nicht weiß, warum ich hier bin
Ich suche nichts bestimmtes
Imagination is an asshole

You're better off
Giving me your girl for the evening
Than your dick
Just sayin'

Bad jokes and psychoanalysis
Kindness
I ran out of stuff to fix at home
Genieß die Sonne!

Interested in people
And cheese...I like cheese

— I'm an Experience

I'm an experience
It appears that I'm very soft
Dysfunctional
Black is my happy color

Schwule Frau interessiert sich für schwule Frauen
Scharmützel
Jetzt bin ich eine Schneelavine
Traveling through jungles

Moron
Equanimous
I will complain about airports
Ask me about my chicken

I'll love your pet more than you
Picture of open mouth with cherry

— I'm the Kind of Girl

I'm the kind of girl
That does a muppet face when angry
I'm either all in
Or don't care at all

Intolerant of close-minded bullshit
Emotionally literate
Zertifizierter Küsser
87kg

Voilà, la réalité!
Beeindruckend anders
Posing in front of bathroom mirror

No couples
No disrespect
No drama

— Ich stehe auf die typische
Rollenverteilung

Ich stehe auf die typische Rollenverteilung
Meistens finde ich Frauen hübscher
In sich selbst
Und dieser irren schönen Welt

I enjoy talking about feelings
Fun sized human
In dubio pro libido
Picture of Gollum

Du hast so viel Stil wie ein Cornetto-Eis
I could cheat on five of you
Henry Miller quote

Kinky, perverse, obszöne und bizarre
Lostplaces
Verlerntes Deutsch

— Not into Politics

Not into politics
A painter
Mostly on a platonic level
Auf eine nackte, kalte Weise interessant

Bonne chance
Sozialer Studienberuf
Proud
But never grown up

Polaroids
Post punk
I am 39
Hoping to have fun

A genius
HAHA

— Funfunfun

Funfunfun
Mich in Hannover rumzuführen
Wobei cool ziemlich subjektiv ist
Entspricht das deinem lahmen leeren Charakter?

Wir stehen auf Primzahlen
Menschen, die gerne staubsaugen
Linksgrünversiffte
Zum Mitzaubern

Somewhere between I want it and I got it
Das kann eine einzige Begegnung bedeuten
The weather is nice
But let's not force it

Keine Zeitverschwendung
Los geht's

— Product of the Cold War Triangle

Product of the Cold War triangle
Necromorphosis
Rub some tiger balm on my back
Wer holt mich hier raus?

Why are you here waiting for a train
Time to live a little
You could have run a hot bath
Read Montaigne

You will strengthen your personality
Besides, it's a lot of fun for everyone involved
Unicorn emoji

Life here is just a test
Don't tell anyone
They might think you're crazy

— Fun Couple

Fun couple
Gerne mal high
Ohne Regenschirm die Welt betreten
And not die frozen

Smartass
Nachtmensch
Talk philosophy is to me
Und dabei nicht nur zusehen

Kitzelschlachten
Boxing glove emoji
I do believe in science
I can't love

Duckface
Das ewige Dilemma

— Academic Slave

Academic slave
Cynical
Lover of penguins
Living kind of fluid

Gute Gespräche
Galactica
Sell the sizzle
Not the sausage

Healthy lifestyle
Anything is a dildo
If you're brave enough

Cheating
Everything you can imagine
Is real

— Ich bin nicht allein hier

Ich bin nicht allein hier
I'm a real joke
Treue Seele
Aber nicht öko

Süße Spielgefährtin
Part-time Politlesbe
À cause de
Piercing im Gesicht

If you're a fridge
Learn German
Warum nicht mal tanzend
Das wäre doch mal ein gutes Lebensziel!

Trümmer
Colonialist vacation selfies

— Rubenesque and Fit

Rubenesque and fit
Looking for »friends«
Ist da irgendwo ein einsamer Cowboy
I have problems with body contact

Soft environment
Very, VERY drug friendly
Bruce Springsteen fan
Dump him

Social media Idiotin
Dogs with short legs
Cinnamon rolls
The sound of silence

Keine Kinder, keine Haustiere
Wer hat Eichhörnchen zu verschenken?

— Sober and Drugfree

Sober and drugfree
New faces and old bars
Overthinking
Getting my life fixed

With a very soft skin
Ich hätte gern für ein paar Stunden
Diese seltene Verknüpfung
Von emotionaler und Intellektueller Verbunden-
    heit

Vanitas
Vanitatum
Et omnia vanitas

Here lies my aspiration
For European features and beauty standards
Explosion emoji

— It's a Trap

It's a trap
Ganz normal aber
Irgendwie doch nicht anders
Funny talk

Multikulti
Normal gestört
The world on the road
Saint Emoji

»Nette Treffen«
Treating people economically
Reden oder trainieren
Picture with snake

Andra tutto bene
Bei mir bist du schön

— Schmeiß die Kinder weg

Schmeiß die Kinder weg
Wir machen neue
Mein Charakter ist konträr
Zu allen stabilen Lebensmodellen

I grow things
Bikes and babes
Büro, Verwaltung
Wohnt in Tharangambadi

Let me cut you gently
Secretly hope that you catch me looking
Picture of dancing on a pole

Looking for a big romance
Open for pretty much everything
In the meantime

— Inhalt

Christian Gohdes

Zivile Seenotrettung auf dem Mittelmeer
Eine Fotoreportage

»Im Mai 2018 rettete die Crew des zivilen Rettungsschiffs Sea-Watch 3 mehr als 460 Menschen vor dem Ertrinken. Während dieser Zeit wurde ich für drei Wochen Teil der Mannschaft und konnte diese Fotodokumentation über Seenotrettung auf dem Mittelmeer erstellen.«
— aus dem Vorwort von Christian Gohdes

64 Seiten, Heft, 978–3–86525–905–9, 10,00 €

80 Seiten, 5 Abb.,
Klappenbroschur
ISBN 978–3–
86525–906–6
10,00 €

Frederik Thiele

wie wir werden
typoskript

Frederik Thiele schreibt Gedichte über die Konsequenzen des Handelns ohne Herzensgüte, mal in verzweifeltem Wimmern, mal in rebellischen Schreien oder betrunkenem Stottern. Die analog auf Schreibmaschine verfassten Texte fokussieren die Offenlegung von emotionalen Prozessen und den Umgang mit psychischen Krankheiten und Traumata. Sie legen ihre Priorität auf die oft vergessene Tugend der Zartheit und die Feinzeichnung des Groben.

_____ / 100